DEUM DE

duration: ca. 10½ minutes

GW00684514

1. JUBILATE D

(1966)

Edition Peters 67322

*piano articulates the beginning of each measure, same chord.

Edition Peters 67322

Subito energico e brutale (slightly faster) (♩ = ♩)

Canon *a 8 voce,* extremely light and ethereal, very smooth (suppress consonants)

* may be done with one or two male voices on each female part and one or two female voices on each male part.   Tessitura may demand the restric-tion to partial sections, e.g., first altos and baritone only.

** alternate version for bass voices: do the part notated for organ pedal, starting where written in the organ part.

*** Piano: L.H. *col' 8va bassa.*

Edition Peters 67322

6

Ju - bi - la - te De-o.

Ju - bi - la-te De-o.

Ju - bi - la-te De-o.

Ju - bi - la-te De-o.

Ju - bi - la - te De - o.

Ju - bi - la - te De-o.

Ju - bi - la - te De-o.

Ju - bi - la - te De-o.

Organ Ped.

Pn. L.H.

Edition Peters 67322

(piano R.H. articulates each measure with chord, as before)

Reverential

S1: Ju - bi - - - la - te _____ De - - - o.

T1: Ju - bi - - - la - te _____ De - - - o.

(tenuto)

(piano *sempre col8va*)

Edition Peters 67322

2. DEO GRATIAS

(for solo soprano or SATB)*

* The entire movement may be done as a solo soprano piece.

Edition Peters 67322

12

Edition Peters 67322

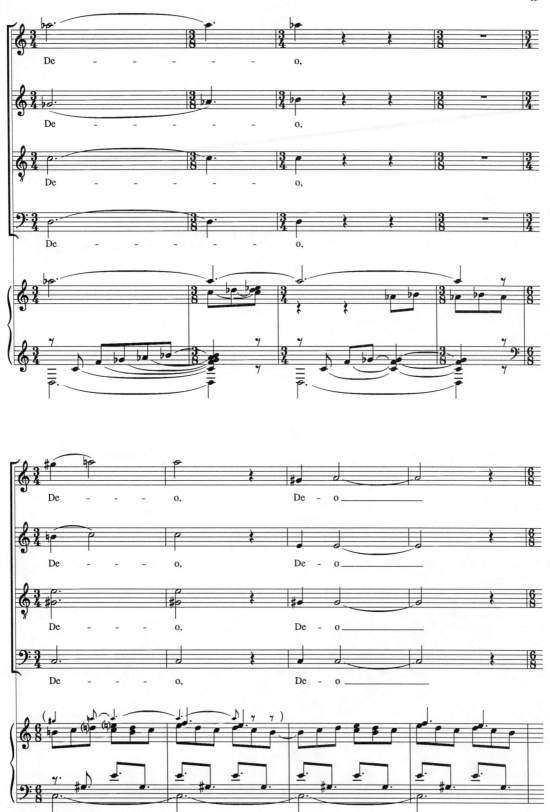

14

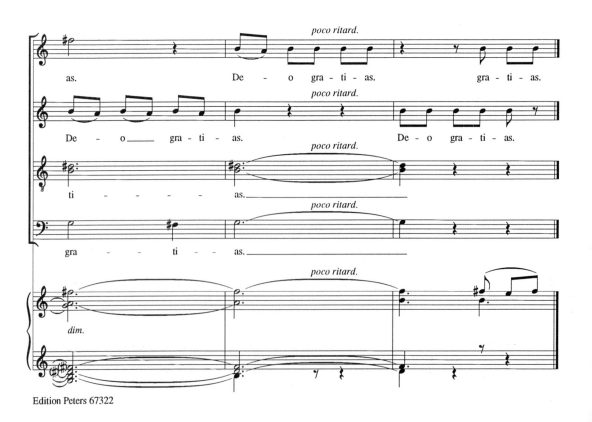

3. GLORIA IN EXCELSIS DEO

* Performance suggestion: all the organ pedal low "C" (𝄢) notes may also be played by a timpani (𝄢) or low drum, ad lib.

Edition Peters 67322

28

(1988)

WILLIAM ALBRIGHT

(continued from back cover)

THE KING OF INSTRUMENTS (A PARADE OF MUSIC AND VERSE) (19 minutes) (P66793)
> Organ Solo and Narrator
> Text: Eugene Haun and William Albright

THE MACHINE AGE (ca. 12 minutes) (P67216)
> Piano Solo

ORGANBOOK III (ca. 28 minutes) (P66794)
> Twelve Etudes for Small Organ

PAX IN TERRA (Latin) (7 minutes) (P66921)
> SATB a cappella
> Text: Biblical

QUINTET FOR CLARINET AND STRING QUARTET (ca. 20 minutes). Score (P67308). Set of Parts (P67038a)

ROMANCE (9 minutes) (P67023)
> French Horn and Organ

SAINTS PRESERVE US (ca. 5 minutes) (P67021)
> Three "Études-prières" for Solo Clarinet

*SEVEN DEADLY SINS (ca. 24 minutes). Score (P66796)
> Flute, Clarinet, String Quartet, Piano, and Optional Narrator
> Text: adapted from Christopher Marlowe's *Doctor Faustus* and William Dunbar's "Dance of the 7 Deadly Sins" (ca. 1500)

SIX NEW HYMNS (ca. 12 minutes) (P66968)
> Unison Chorus and Organ

SONATA FOR ALTO SAXOPHONE AND PIANO (ca. 20 minutes) (P67101)

*A SONG TO DAVID (60 minutes) (P67020)
> Antiphonal Choirs, Soloists and Organ
> Text: Christopher Smart (18th Century)

*SPHAERA (ca. 13 minutes) (P67085)
> Piano and Computer-generated 4-channel Tape

SYMPHONY FOR ORGAN (ca. 30 minutes) (P67162)
> Organ Solo with Percussion (or Pre-recorded Tape)

TAKE UP THE SONG (8½ minutes) (P67263)
> Soprano Solo, Mixed Chorus and Piano
> Text: Edna St. Vincent Millay

THAT SINKING FEELING... (Morceau de concours) (ca. 5 minutes) (P67022)
> Organ Solo

THREE NEW CHESTNUTS (ca. 10 minutes) (P67163)
> Two Harpsichords

THREE ORIGINAL RAGS (11 minutes) (P66920)
> Piano Solo

1732: IN MEMORIAM JOHANNES ALBRECHT (ca. 15 minutes) (P67129)
> Organ Solo

*performance material available on rental

WILLIAM ALBRIGHT

ABIDING PASSIONS (ca. 15½ minutes). Score (P67390). Set of Parts (P67390a)
Fl, Ob, Cl (A), Bsn, Hrn

ANTIGONE'S REPLY (ca. 5 minutes) (P67291)
Sop, Bar Soli, SATB, Pf
Text: Sophocles

*BACCHANAL (15 minutes) (P66918)
Organ Solo, 3(Picc)3(EH)3(E♭, Bcl)3(Cbsn) 4431 T, Perc(3), Hp, Cel, Str (Cbcl ad lib)

CHASM (10½ minutes) (P67160)
Organ (with optional "echo" instrument)

*CHASM (SYMPHONIC FRAGMENT) (ca. 11 minutes) (P67315)
3(Picc)3(EH)3(Bcl)3(Cbsn) Alto Sax 4431 T, Perc(3), Pf, Hp, Str

CHICHESTER MASS (ca. 8 minutes) (P66795)
SATB a cappella
Text: Ordinary of Mass (English)

*CONCERTO FOR HARPSICHORD AND STRINGS (ca. 28 minutes) (P67458)

DAVID'S SONGS (9½ minutes) (P66969)
SATB Soloists or Chorus and Organ
Text: Psalm 149: 1-3; 116: 1-6; 137: 1-2; 150

DE SPIRITUM (20 minutes) (P67161)
Organ Solo with two assistants

DEUM DE DEO (ca. 10½ minutes) (P67322)
SATB, Org/Pf

THE ENIGMA SYNCOPATIONS (24 minutes). Score (P67081). Set of Parts (P67081a)
Fl, Cb, Perc, Org

FIVE CHROMATIC DANCES (28 minutes) (P66797)
Piano Solo

FOUR FANCIES (12 minutes) (P67128)
Harpsichord Solo

HALO (7 minutes) (P66798)
Organ Solo and Metal Instruments (1 player)

HYMNS AND DESCANTS FROM "A SONG TO DAVID" (10 minutes) (P67020a)
Mixed Chorus (Congregation) and Organ
Text: Christopher Smart (18th Century)

*INTRODUCTION, PASSACAGLIA AND RONDO CAPRICCIOSO (14 minutes) (P66919)
Tack Pf, Fl, Cl, Alto Sax, Hrn, Trp, Trb, Tba, Perc

JERICHO (ca. 15 minutes) (P66825)
Battle Music for Trumpet and Organ

(continued inside)

*performance material available on rental

ISBN 9790300738239
DEUM DE DEO
90000

9 790300 738239